MONEY MAGIC

MONEY MAGIC

*Attracting prosperity and abundance
into your life and home*

Antonia Beattie

PARKGATE
BOOKS

CONTENTS

CONTENTS

INTRODUCTION —
PROSPERITY AND ABUNDANCE

The ability to control the flow of prosperity and abundance in our endeavors is one of the most important factors in allowing us to feel secure and nurtured. How we gain such control has been the intention of a number of incantations, spells, amulets and talismans devised since ancient times.

Extraordinary tales have been told through the centuries of magicians paying an innkeeper for their food and board with gold that turned into dust once they had left the inn. Many an alchemist believed that he could be wealthy beyond his wildest dreams if only he could find the elusive Philosopher's Stone, a substance reputed to have the power to turn ordinary cheap metal into precious gold.

Very much as in real life, folk tales in virtually all cultures abound with tales of the pitfalls of trying to find an easy way of making money. Often it is not as easy as it sounds, such as trying to find the end of the rainbow to dig up a pot of fairy gold. Finding the end of the rainbow seems an easy task, until we try to actually pinpoint the spot.

Many spells, incantations and charms were aimed not only at the acquisition of money and possessions but also at the protection of wealth already amassed. Both attraction and protection spells were generally based on the assumption that the distribution of wealth was essentially in the hands of fate, often personified as Lady Luck. Yet, even with gambling, the right information can give you the power to make your abundance materialize despite the apparent fickleness of fate.

This book is designed to give you the information you need to help even up the odds. Oftentimes, what we think of as fate working in our favor or to our detriment is really the effect of the planets, phases of the moon and the cycles of the season. In money magic, understanding such cycles of the outside world is as important as understanding the rises and falls of the economic climate.

Any spells that attract wealth and abundance are a form of money magic. As with any form of magic, you only get out of it what you put in, with focus being one of the most important keys to abundance. By learning to focus your thoughts and by working with your intuition, you can effectively manifest for yourself an extremely prosperous and happy future and not some empty pot at the bottom of a fading rainbow.

THE BASICS OF MONEY MAGIC

WHAT IS MONEY MAGIC?

Money magic is a collection of magical practices and techniques that can help you attract wealth, prosperity and good luck into your life and the lives of your loved ones. This form of magic works irrespective of the financial climate around you because the magic operates through you and what you believe you can do.

Money magic works on many levels. Exercises are included that help you tap into your intuition about your financial circumstances. If you want help to understand why your finances are in the state they are in, divination techniques such as astrology, the Tarot, numerology and the *I Ching* can be very useful.

In Western magic there is a strong belief in cycles and the benefits of attuning ourselves to the cycles of nature and the universe. According to this theory, you might be spending too much energy trying to counter-balance the effects of your unfavorable circumstances when you should instead be learning an important lesson. That lesson could be to understand the cycles of the planets and the seasons and to learn to flow with both the ups and downs of life, or it may be that you need to face a personal fear, or rectify a particular habit that keeps getting you into the same troublesome situation with issues of prosperity. What you really need is more information to understand the cycles of your life and to help you choose the optimum times for working money magic.

HOW DOES IT WORK?

Money magic is sometimes the hardest magic to manifest for ourselves, because we often encounter deeply held beliefs that a desire for money makes us greedy or that we don't deserve to be comfortable

or prosperous. For quicker results, consider working with a group of friends, casting spells for each other. For longer lasting and much more personally satisfying results, learn to conquer any pertinent self-defeating feelings and discover your own individual path to abundance. There is no "right" way to practice money magic.

However, money magic generally works most powerfully when you are able to tune into:

- your true will;
- your intuition;
- your belief that you can make a difference; and
- your insights concerning your own financial circumstances.

You are then in a much better position to cast successful money magic spells or visualize your own form of prosperity and abundance. One of the most important aspects of Western magic is its emphasis on the need to follow your true will. In many magical traditions, a person's true will is always attuned to his or her greater good, and not toward following any whim or fancy.

Money magic is, above all, not about greed. This emotion is not usually felt by a person who seeks abundance or prosperity in line with his or her sense of the greater good. Greed often indicates an unconscious conviction that wealth is unattainable or undeserved. For this reason, many traditional magical spells do not work if greed is the prime motivating force. Money spells generally work successfully only when a person seeks to fulfill his or her immediate need.

WHAT IS LUCK? — THE GOOD, THE BAD AND THE UGLY

The concept of "luck" is based on the belief that fortunes can be either amassed or destroyed purely by chance. Since ancient times, a certain set of symbols has gained the reputation of being magically able to attract good luck while another complementary set of symbols, which were reputedly able to repel bad luck, has developed. Philosophers, through the centuries, have questioned whether these images actually worked, arguing about the impossibility of measuring a symbol's power to deflect bad luck.

Whether or not a symbol works as a good luck charm relates to how strongly a person believes in the inherent power of that image. The force of such a belief can create its own magic (see pages 46–51).

SPECIFIC CHINESE SYMBOLS FOR GOOD FORTUNE, WEALTH, SUCCESS OR POWER

Animals: bats, deer, unicorn
Fish: any, but particularly goldfish
Flowers: any, but particularly the peony
Colors: orange, gold
Other images: coins, house, water

There is another equally valid way to view luck. It has often been remarked that people who are wholeheartedly following their true calling in life seem to be lucky in that they appear to attract greater opportunities and financial rewards. This harmonization of financial support and the following of one's true path is often based on a person's intuition (see pages 24–31), and their understanding of the cycles of the world around them. Good luck may also merely be a person's finely tuned ability to recognize and take opportunities when they arise.

Feelings of bad luck may be diverted by first placing faith in a good luck symbol that resonates for you. This can buy you some breathing space to sort out what you really should be doing and to assess the values you place on having more than a comfortable amount of money. You may also choose to look at whether what you really want is not so much the money but a happy and fulfilled life. A string of bad luck experiences can be a clear indication that there is a challenge in your life that you may not be addressing yet. You may find that once that central challenge is faced, your luck will change.

SPELLCRAFT

Money spells, like many other areas of magic work, require the observance of a number of important "rules" so that the spell has the best chance of working for you.

Rule 1

Work out whether you need the money itself or whether you really want a particular thing, such as a comfortable home. Sometimes, spells work in mysterious ways. For example, you may wish for a roomy, beautiful home with a lush garden, which you know will require a certain amount of money to achieve. However, a spell directed toward the object you really desire does not necessarily mean that you have to invoke money into your life — the house could come to you in other ways, such as an unexpected inheritance.

Rule 2

Set reasonable parameters around your desire. It is important that you can gain confidence in your ability to make things happen by force of your will and your intuition.

Rule 3

Decide how much you really need. Spells often work only if the spell is aimed at fulfilling your real needs.

Rule 4

Be specific in what you want. Remember, there are no limits on how many money spells you perform. So set out your priorities. What is your most pressing need at the moment?

Rule 5

Believe that the spell will work. Remember that spells are a powerful way of focusing your mind for a particular purpose. They set up a path for you to find the wealth or possessions that you need (see pages 54–55).

CANDLE MAGIC

Candle magic is a form of spell in which an appropriately colored, lighted candle is used to help you focus on what you wish to happen, say, the acquisition of a sum of money to pay off your credit cards.

For money magic, green candles are traditionally used. However, feel free to choose any other color for your candle, according to your intuition or particular associations. For example, you may wish to find the money for your education and could then choose a color for your candle that reflects to you your chosen career.

Once you have chosen the color of your candle, purchase or make the candle with your intention in mind. You must dedicate your purpose to the candle and make sure you use it for no other reason. In order to prepare your candles, focus on your purpose and anoint the candle by rubbing some oil on it and, if you wish, carving a simple word or symbol to sum up your purpose down the side of the candle.

Place your candle onto or into a safe receptacle and light it, again while thinking of your purpose. Once the wick is lit you may allow the candle to burn itself out in an empty bath tub or safe tiled area. While the flame is burning down the candle, your wish is streaming into the air for however long the candle takes to burn completely down.

YOUR INTUITION

Gut reactions, hunches, an instinctive "feeling" — these are all terms that refer to your intuition. Intuition is a rapid and seemingly irrational mental process that is invaluable in the practice of any form of magic.

One of the best ways of tapping into your intuitive abilities is to create a safe and quiet haven, within which you can sit quietly and listen to your inner voice. This is a form of meditation which you can use to focus on a particular issue that concerns you financially.

It is important to first find a quiet space where you will not be disturbed for at least an hour. If you are feeling especially harassed by your financial problem, imagine a circle of blue light surrounding you, shutting out the everyday world. Feel that that world is receding and is merely a shadow. Sit or lie comfortably in this special space and begin to concentrate on your breathing. For ideas to help you sink deeper into your meditation, see page 26. Allow everyday thoughts to drift out of your mind.

When ready, concentrate on a financial issue, such as "How do I find financial fulfillment?" Ask only one question per session. Focus on this question and allow thoughts to come to you. It is particularly important to feel detached and calm about your question and to refrain from judging or criticizing the thoughts that float to the surface.

When you feel ready to emerge from your meditation, concentrate on your breathing and become conscious of your special space. If you have encircled your area with blue light, remember to "shut off" the light before leaving your space. Keep a journal handy and jot down the impressions that came to you and see how to incorporate any solutions given into your life.

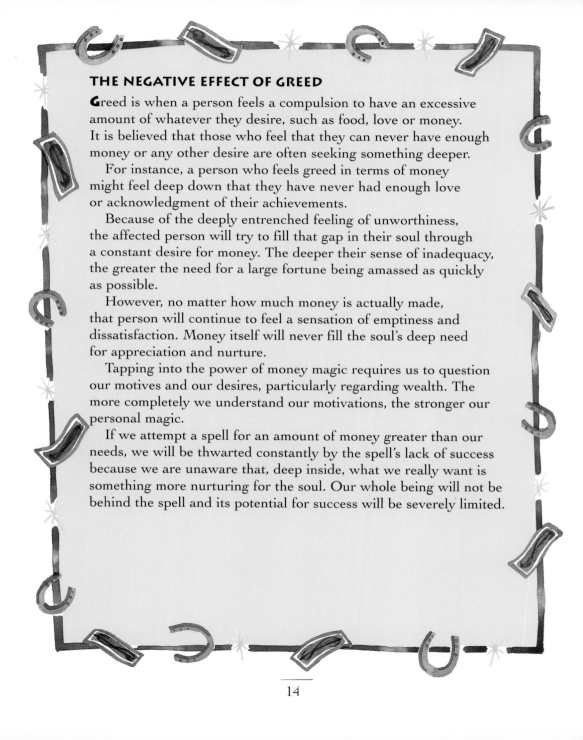

THE NEGATIVE EFFECT OF GREED

Greed is when a person feels a compulsion to have an excessive amount of whatever they desire, such as food, love or money. It is believed that those who feel that they can never have enough money or any other desire are often seeking something deeper.

For instance, a person who feels greed in terms of money might feel deep down that they have never had enough love or acknowledgment of their achievements.

Because of the deeply entrenched feeling of unworthiness, the affected person will try to fill that gap in their soul through a constant desire for money. The deeper their sense of inadequacy, the greater the need for a large fortune being amassed as quickly as possible.

However, no matter how much money is actually made, that person will continue to feel a sensation of emptiness and dissatisfaction. Money itself will never fill the soul's deep need for appreciation and nurture.

Tapping into the power of money magic requires us to question our motives and our desires, particularly regarding wealth. The more completely we understand our motivations, the stronger our personal magic.

If we attempt a spell for an amount of money greater than our needs, we will be thwarted constantly by the spell's lack of success because we are unaware that, deep inside, what we really want is something more nurturing for the soul. Our whole being will not be behind the spell and its potential for success will be severely limited.

THE POWER OF FAIRY GOLD

There are many myths and legends about the fairy folk, particularly concerning their helpfulness to people in distress and to those who are kind. However, the fairies can be merciless to individuals who display a greedy nature.

One story relates how the fairies helped a young man who faced eviction from his home by an evil, miserly man who refused to give the young man an extension within which to repay a loan. The young man, who had a growing family, had been falling behind in his mortgage repayments. The fellow had spent many sleepless nights trying to work out how to get out of debt. One evening, as he could not sleep, the young man took a walk through the moonlit forest to sit by a lake and ponder his fate.

As he stared moodily into the dark waters, a tall apparition loomed up from the lake and sat beside him. The young man had grown up with legends about this apparition, the King of the Lake Fairies, so he did not run away. Instead, upon the King's request, the young man told him his sad story.

The King listened carefully and, at the end of the young man's tale, he stood and made a shrill noise. All of a sudden, bright jewel-like fairies began to troop from the lake, laden with gold coins. The King warned the young man that the coins must only be paid toward the mortgage and that the young man should be careful to get a receipt.

Later that morning, the young man took the gold to the miser and paid out his entire mortgage. The miser handed the young man the receipt, and with no uncertain glee went back to his safe to look at the gold that he had never expected to see. To his great consternation, he found that the gold had turned into gray, worthless pebbles.

The young man continued to prosper and every year he gave thanks to the King of the Lake Fairies by keeping the shores of the lake clean and by raising his glass silently every May Day to toast the King.

HELP FROM ABOVE AND BEYOND

THE EFFECT OF THE PLANETS

Since about 3000 B.C., human civilization has observed that the movement of the heavenly bodies correspond to twelve different types of people. The characteristics of each type of person are, according to astrology, linked to the twelve constellations of the zodiac. Which sign or character type you are depends on which constellation the sun was passing on the day of your birth. These characteristics cover many aspects of human behavior, including how a sun sign deals with money.

The movement of the planets through the zodiac do not necessarily determine our inescapable fate, but indicate certain behavioral patterns that can be modified by our will. For instance, knowing that your sun sign is impulsive concerning money can lead you to develop a way of making sure that in the future you double check any dealings involving substantial sums of money.

A number of planets have also been assigned a certain form of energy which you can tap into for spellcraft. For instance, money magic spells are best performed on Thursday, the day ruled by Jupiter.

The following chart gives you a brief guide to the twelve sun signs and their abilities to handle money. Do not feel concerned if some of the descriptions do not appear to suit you; you may already have changed your strategies around money from past experience, or the way you handle or perceive money may have been overlaid by your parents' philosophies about money and abundance. If you were born near the cusp of two signs, i.e. near when one sign ends and another begins, check the descriptions for both sun signs.

WHAT SUN SIGN ARE YOU? MONETARY ABILITIES

Aries *March 20 to April 20*	*You can make good money from entrepreneurial enterprises but need to watch out for impulsive decisions and the need for quick returns.*
Taurus *April 21 to May 21*	*You are very competent financially and tend to seek secure investments.*
Gemini *May 22 to June 21*	*You are safer making money through spreading your money over a number of different types of investments to counter boredom.*
Cancer *June 22 to July 22*	*You are good at keeping hold of money and are careful in your investments portfolio, having an aversion to taking risks.*
Leo *July 23 to August 23*	*You are interested in making money through high quality investments and tend to spend more money than you ought on your home.*
Virgo *August 24 to September 23*	*You are hardworking and meticulous in your acquisition of wealth and tend to be careful with your investments.*
Libra *September 24 to October 23*	*You are interested in making money in partnership with another person but often need to seek the help of a professional financial adviser to diversify your finances.*
Scorpio *October 24 to November 23*	*You are able to invest and make money shrewdly and creatively with a great deal of common sense.*
Sagittarius *November 24 to December 21*	*You are often bored by money and tend to invest to support development of a product rather than to make money.*
Capricorn *December 22 to January 20*	*You are careful with money and have an ability to make the most of the money you make.*
Aquarius *January 21 to February 18*	*You are often prone to gambling with your money or putting all your investments into one venture.*
Pisces *February 19 to March 19*	*You are a bit careless with money and should seek the help of a financial adviser to guide you in terms of your investments.*

THE POWER OF THE MOON

The symbol of the new moon, the crescent, was thought to be lucky because it was symbolic of new promise and growth. The phase of a new moon is a perfect time to seek aid and guidance about a new project, business relationship or career move.

The energy at new moon is young, wild, strong and undirected. This is an excellent time to focus your will on what you want to happen concerning your financial projects or circumstances and to mold a new path for yourself, using this powerful form of energy. This is the time to allow your ideas to take seed, no matter how fantastic or ambitious. Anything can happen once you have sown the seeds of your will, using new moon energy.

Sometimes knowing which ideas to go with can be difficult, and you may also wish to seek guidance from the new energy of the moon. On the night of a new moon, write down each of your various potential ideas on a separate piece of paper. One of the possibilities should be that you haven't as yet identified your best solution.

Find a comfortable space where you can see the moon — it does not matter whether you are outside or inside. It is important to feel safe and that you will not be disturbed. Show each piece of paper to the moon and then fold it twice, so that you do not see the writing. Place the folded pieces of paper onto the floor at your feet and shuffle them around so that you lose track of your choices.

Concentrate on the moon and her energy. As the energy at new moon is undirected, use your imagination to mold this energy

18

into a strong, concentrated beam of light, which is searching through a myriad of possibilities at your feet. Imagine the beam alighting upon one of the pieces of paper. Pick up the piece of paper and see what path has been chosen.

It is important to feel comfortable about that choice. Before taking any action, take time to do a meditation on the chosen decision. Sit in quietness and clear your head of any extraneous thoughts. Allow your mind to just focus on the chosen decision and allow thoughts about the decision to filter into your mind. When ready, emerge from your meditation and write your thoughts down in a journal. This is particularly useful if the moonbeam chose the piece of paper indicating that you have to think of a new direction.

Remember, that when doing any working with the moon, you should always thank the moon for her help. You may also obtain a moon blessing for your project's successful outcome.

MONEY MAGIC MOON SPELL

At new moon, empty all the money out of your wallet or purse. Show the money you have in your wallet to the moon, imagining that as the moon increases or waxes, so too will the amount of money you have. This is a variation on a traditional spell of turning the money in your pocket over the first time you see the new moon.

THE ENERGY OF THE SEASONS

In many of the ancient systems, there is a belief that the world is made up of a number of elements and that their energy is linked with the birth, growth and death of the earth's energies as marked by the seasons. In traditional Chinese thinking, the world is made up of five elements — fire, earth, metal, water and wood — and each has its particular effect on the cycle of the seasons and the flow of your finances.

The season of spring is linked with the element of wood. The energy in this season is highly unpredictable and unstable but filled with enormous enthusiasm and a feeling of great potential. You might find that your finances are in a state of flux with tremendous highs and lows. It is a time of new ideas and the possibilities of new ventures.

Spring is a very risky time — you may find that you are able to make a large sum of money quickly, but you may also lose all that money just as fast. There is no sense of consistency during this season but it is a good time to sow the seeds for a longer term project because, as the energies are so scattered, you will be able to impose your will more effectively.

The season of summer is linked with the element of fire. The energy is maturing and intensifying. You will find that you start to get consistent returns on the money you have invested or that more possibilities for making money come to fruition. This is a very social time and you will find that the people with whom you are in contact may give you more opportunities and hints for making money. This is a good time to make hay while the sun shines.

The season of late summer in the Chinese system, which is the shortest season of the year, is linked with the element of earth. In the Northern Hemisphere, the season occurs between 31 July and the autumn equinox in mid September. In the Southern Hemisphere, it occurs between the 31 January and the autumn equinox in mid March. It is believed that this is the most balanced time of the year, when money flow is unimpeded and opportunities and successful outcomes are at their optimum.

The energy is the balance between the first harvest and the last fruiting. If you find that you are not experiencing financial success during this time, it might be an idea to examine whether you have planted all the ideas and followed up all the opportunities of which you were capable. Make notes on the problems you experienced and when you encountered them, and work toward having a better late summer harvest in the next cycle.

The season of autumn is linked with the element of metal. The seasonal energy is becoming introverted. There is a final gathering of the energy, but be careful to store a large part of it for the winter months. Save some of the money you have made during late summer and autumn to tide you over winter. This is the time for consolidation.

The season of winter is linked with the element of water. During this time, energy is being conserved. However, although the energy has gone underground, there is still growth going on beneath the Earth's surface. This is the time to start planning for the next cycle of the year. It is the time to assimilate all the lessons you have learnt during the previous cycle and to devise new plans, possibly using some of the leftover wealth you have amassed.

THE WISDOM OF YOUR NATURE SPIRIT GUIDES

According to Native American beliefs, we can gain enormous wisdom and guidance from the natural world, from entities such as tree spirits, as well as bird and animal spirits (see page 49 for information about animal images).

If you are feeling upset about your financial situation, consider taking a walk in nature. The sheer act of walking on the earth, especially in bare feet, is excellent for linking into a feeling of being grounded, of being linked into the earth energy.

In both Native American and Celtic traditions, observing nature is seen as a wonderful way to gain answers to your financial questions. Before you go for your walk in nature, partake of a light meal, including some vegetable juice, and abstain from coffee, tea and sweets. Take some pure water with you and a backpack so that your hands are free and you feel balanced while walking. On a longer walk, it is always sensible to wear good walking shoes so that your feet feel comfortable, leaving your mind free to watch the world around you.

Before your walk, focus on the one pressing financial issue that is disturbing you. When you walk out of the door to your house or your car, discipline yourself not to think about your problem during the entire walk. Instead, focus on observing the natural world around you. What shapes are the clouds in the sky? Are there birds flying overhead? Is there any wildlife scurrying around?

Any activity that catches your eye should be carefully observed. A small creature gathering seeds for storage may indicate that you may need to gather your energies as a solution to your problems. The number of birds flying overhead may indicate a lucky number.

If going out on a walk through the forest or bush, always make sure to tell someone where you are going or in what area you anticipate exploring. Sometimes, if you are walking in fairly rugged terrain, it is a good idea to inform the police about your walking plans.

Sometimes on your walk, you may come across a bird feather. Pick the feather up and stroke it, imagining the bird flying freely and happily. Allow the free energy of the bird to enter your soul through your hands as you hold the feather. Listen to the thoughts that drift through your mind. A little bird spirit may well be trying to tell you how you could also achieve a similar sense of freedom.

It is also not unknown for tree leaves to spiral into your hand, sometimes even if your hand is in your pocket. Take the hint. If you can see the tree from which the leaf has dropped, go to it and, if possible, sit within its roots or stand touching its trunk. It may also have a message for you, particularly if you need to solve your problem by finding more stability in your life.

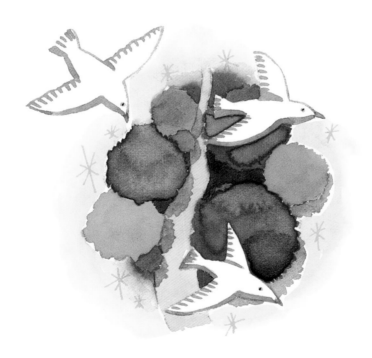

GETTING IN TOUCH WITH YOUR INTUITION

ALLOWING YOURSELF TO FEEL ABUNDANT — DEVELOPING A SENSE OF HOPE

Often our own negative feelings can get in the way of both our prosperity and our intuition. If we do not believe that we can be prosperous in our life, then no money spell in the world can change our financial circumstances.

To help charge your emotions with a new feeling of hope, consider doing the following exercise. Find a quiet, comfortable spot where you will not be disturbed. You will need to be able to sit as close to the ground as possible, while still being comfortable. You will also need a green-colored stone that appeals to you — try malachite, jade, raw emerald, green tourmaline or peridot. Some of these can be purchased fairly inexpensively, especially if the stone is small, uncut or unpolished.

The exercise involves visualizing a strong symbol of hope, such as a flourishing oak tree. The energy of the tree, like that of the earth, goes through cycles of birth, death and rebirth. If you are feeling that things are hopeless concerning your financial circumstances, you may wish to start your visualization of the oak tree as bare and bereft of any leaves, as it is in the middle of winter.

Imagine that the tree and you are one. Feel that your branches are vulnerable and exposed to the storms and winds. See if these feelings resonate with the way you feel about your finances. Do you feel at the mercy of financial institutions, the economy or other circumstances out of your control? To counter this, feel that your trunk is extending down deep into the earth. The deeper your roots go down, the warmer and more vibrant the energy you feel. Allow this feeling to come through your feet and trunk into the center of your body's energy, about three fingers below your navel.

When you are ready, see that the wind has dropped around your tree and that the sun is beginning to shine through your branches. Feel that deep earth energy start to flow up your roots. Feel the energy shimmer up and down your trunk and branches and see little light green buds emerge on your branches. Feel the excitement of new life coming into your center.

Allow the energy of newness to swirl in the center of your being. Take your green-colored stone and place it over your center. Sense some of the energy entering into your stone as you keep it positioned over your center. Green-colored stones are noted for their traditional resonance with prosperity magic.

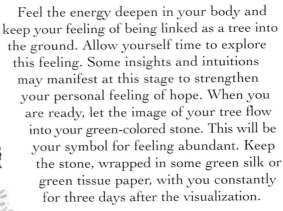

Feel the energy deepen in your body and keep your feeling of being linked as a tree into the ground. Allow yourself time to explore this feeling. Some insights and intuitions may manifest at this stage to strengthen your personal feeling of hope. When you are ready, let the image of your tree flow into your green-colored stone. This will be your symbol for feeling abundant. Keep the stone, wrapped in some green silk or green tissue paper, with you constantly for three days after the visualization.

RELAXATION TECHNIQUES — IMPROVING CIRCULATION INSIDE AND AROUND YOU

To be able to link into our intuition we must also be able to release the stress we feel in our bodies. Often, when we feel physically unfit and tired there is a decrease in the energy circulating not only in our bodies but our lives as well. If we think of financial prosperity as a form of energy, by increasing the circulation within your body, you are also creating space for the circulation of financial energy. As your circulation improves, your body will feel more and more relaxed because it is no longer having to do extra work to deal with stagnant energies. Similarly, as your energy increases, you will be able to attract similar energy, such as financial stability or abundance.

An excellent exercise to help energy circulate through your body is to breathe new energy into your tan tien. In ancient Chinese beliefs, the tan tien is the center of your body and can be found about three fingers below your navel. To tap into its power, stand straight with your feet hip-width apart and place your hands just below your navel. Once you are feeling balanced, breathe through your nose into your tan tien. Feel your abdomen expand. Imagine new, clean energy coming into your body through your nose and lungs and into your tan tien. As you breath out, visualize the energy looping around your navel and traveling back up through the lungs and nose. Know that the energy that is being exhaled contains stagnant energy and any unhappy feelings and stresses.

Practice this exercise daily, learning to breath this way for up to five minutes at one session. Consider doing this exercise as soon as you wake in the morning. You will feel more and more relaxed, and soon you will find that your intuition will return with renewed vigor and you will be able to find new opportunities for feeling prosperous in the world.

To help relax your body and to liven up your energy, do not forget to do these simple everyday tasks:
- *walk once a day, everyday, at the same time and for the same duration (preferably in the morning); and*
- *take some time, at least ten minutes, in the evening to sit quietly and empty your mind of all thoughts of the day.*

LEARNING TO LISTEN TO YOUR INTUITION

> *"The end of chaos is the beginning of prosperity"*
> ***I Ching*** *(from hexagram No. 18, Kû)*

Learning to listen to our intuition is a two stage exercise. First, we must remove the clutter that surrounds our everyday life and makes it difficult to listen to our inner voice. Second, we must trust in what this voice tells us.

In feng shui, the ancient Chinese art of design and placement, it is believed that clutter must be eliminated in our homes and workplaces to enable the proper flow of beneficial energy through our homes, offices and lives. The same principle applies to our minds, which are constantly in action, thinking, synthesizing information, storing impressions.

By working out what we want (in this context, financially), our intuition may help us prioritize what we need to do and when. Often, by being specific about your needs, it becomes easier to hear your intuition. You are creating a space within your mind to hear new thoughts. This will make it easier to be more creative in your thinking — to feel that you can indeed solve your financial problems, through both conventional and non-conventional means.

You may find it useful to set yourself a series of questions to help clarify your financial needs and wishes, such as the following:

- How much money do I need?
- How much money do I want?
- What do I want to do with the money?
- Are these wishes my own or someone else's?
- What would happen if my wishes did/did not come true?
- How would I feel?

It is important to keep in mind that the simple acquisition of money or financial security cannot buy you the true love or respect of another person, nor can it make you feel secure within yourself.

Set a time and select a special space in which you feel that you are apart from the world to ask yourself these questions and to evaluate what you need and want. Once you have set the scene, your intuition will be able to provide you with many of the answers you are seeking.

When you feel your intuition is at work, try to do your best to follow your own advice. Remember a time when you had similar feelings — were you right? Or were your thoughts echoing a fear rather than assessing the current situation? The best way to cope with the manifestation of an old fear is to do some self-analysis to understand what your fears are in this area and whether they are appropriate to your present situation — self-knowledge gives you power.

GAZING INTO A PROSPEROUS FUTURE — SCRYING

Scrying is a form of divination, which interprets images or symbols that appear to form through a mist in a quartz crystal or Perspex ball, a bowl of water or through the smoke rising from a cauldron or fireplace.

Although since medieval times the visions seen from scrying were thought by some to be messages from evil spirits, many now realize that scrying was indeed an excellent way of linking into the subconscious mind.

A fire scrying is most suitable for a prosperity working. You will need a metal bowl (preferably bronze) which should be about 12 inches (30 cm) wide and at least 8 inches (20 cm) deep. Fill a third of the bowl with sand. You may set a coin (traditionally one you have already won) into the sand and use it afterward as a prosperity amulet. Construct a layer of twisted paper (maybe using "pretend" money made from recycled paper) and cover the layer of paper with small twigs. Place the cauldron on the floor, preferably on a number of loose ceramic tiles. Sit in front of the cauldron on the floor with your box of matches, pen, journal and a glass of your favorite spirit, such as scotch or brandy. Before you light the cauldron, dedicate the purpose of your scrying by sipping some of your spirits. Then pour the rest of the liquid onto the twigs (experiment with the amount of alcohol needed to start the fire but be very careful and begin with a small quantity first). If you do not drink alcohol, use commercial fire-starters.

The purpose of the scrying in money magic terms is to work out how to obtain a prosperous future. Keeping that purpose in mind, light the fire while repeating in your head or out loud the following mantra or one that you have composed:

Let this fire
Visions inspire

Once the flames start to swirl in the cauldron, gaze into them as you continue to say your mantra. Scrying involves relaxing the muscles of your eyes so that as you concentrate your vision remains slightly unfocused. Eventually shapes and patterns will emerge in the flames or smoke, revealing a symbol, number or a picture. This might be your lucky number, or the symbol might be one that brings you a sense of confidence in business.

Allow time for the symbol, numbers or pictures to emerge. Do not be frightened, but stay with what your subconscious is saying to you. If the symbols are unfamiliar, you may need to do some research into what they might mean.

Even if the images make no sense whatsoever to you, note them down. Allow yourself about ten to fifteen minutes for your first scrying session. Continue scrying once a week (preferably on a Thursday) and you will find that you are given more and more information. Work with it and you will be richly rewarded.

SOME MONEY MAGIC SYMBOLS

Four leaf clover: *unexpected monetary success*
Upright horseshoe: *good luck*
Key: *golden opportunities*
Doorway: *promotion*
Knife: *betrayal*

FORTUNE TELLING

CHINESE ASTROLOGY — ANIMAL WISDOM

In Western astrology, the month within which a person was born was believed to determine the person's general destiny and character traits. In Chinese astrology, the year, as opposed to the month, of birth is seen to have this same effect on a person's fate. The Chinese believe in the Great Year. This is a twelve-year cycle, each year having a particular energy relating to the turn of events, the personalities of those born during that year, and other aspects such as luck and prosperity.

By the eight or ninth century A.D., a group of twelve animals evolved which were believed to epitomize the qualities of each of the twelve years in the Great Year cycle, the first year being the Year of the Rat and the twelfth year being the Year of the Pig. Each year in the cycle also has a particular energy concerning business and finances.

Those who are born in a certain cycle of the Great Year will enjoy good fortune each time that point in the cycle recurs. For instance, those born in the Year of the Dragon will find that they have particularly prosperous times during subsequent Years of the Dragon in each twelve year cycle. To find out what animal sign you are, check the table on pages 75–77, and see within which period your birthday falls and what animal influences future years. You may also wish to use the image of your Chinese astrological animal as a good luck charm (see pages 50–51) or in your protection amulet (see pages 72–73).

The following table gives a brief description of the type of financial year that can be expected when influenced by a particular animal. The table also gives an indication whether the year is especially profitable or unprofitable for people born under certain animal signs. Check the table on pages 75–77 to work out which animal is dominant in a particular year, and read the financial trends of that year in the table below.

Year of the Rat

As the Year of the Rat is the beginning of a new twelve-year cycle, this year promises opportunities to start new ventures and businesses. This is the time to sow the seeds for future prosperity. It is an auspicious time for the Rat, Tiger, Dragon, Snake, Monkey and Dog, but a potentially troublesome time for the Hare, Sheep, Rooster and Pig.

ANCIENT WISDOM

If you see a well fed rat unexpectedly turn up in your home, take it as a sign of future prosperity.

Year of the Ox

Develop the projects you have started last year or consolidate your position. This is not a good time to start new ventures unless you are able to complete them within the same year. Investigate stable investments and do not go into risky propositions. This is a year of stability. It is an auspicious time for the Rat, Ox, Snake and Pig, but a potentially troublesome time for the Tiger, Hare, Dragon, Sheep and Dog.

Year of the Tiger

This is an unpredictable year with a number of upheavals and changes. It is best not to enter into any risky ventures and to be prepared for unexpected turns, not necessarily for the worse. It is an auspicious time for the Rat, Ox, Tiger, Hare, Dragon, Horse and Dog, but a potentially troublesome time for the Snake, Monkey and Pig.

Year of the Hare

This is a peaceful and stable year with opportunities arising for joint ventures and the further development of business ideas. It is a time for consolidation and for strengthening your financial position. It is an auspicious time for the Ox, Hare, Snake, Dog and Pig, but a potentially troublesome time for the Rat, Dragon, Monkey and Rooster.

Year of the Dragon

The time is ripe for the start of adventurous and imaginative business plans. This is a year of great ups and downs. It is an auspicious time for the Rat, Tiger, Dragon, Snake and Horse, but a potentially troublesome time for the Ox, Hare and Sheep.

Year of the Snake

Watching your back in finance and business is the key to survival during this year. This is not a good time to start any new ventures. It is an auspicious time for the Ox, Hare, Snake, Sheep and Rooster, but a potentially troublesome time for the Rat, Ox, Tiger, Monkey, Dog and Pig.

Year of the Horse

This is a year of surprises, large scale changes and a good time for expansion. It is an auspicious time for the Tiger, Dragon, Horse, Sheep and Dog, but a potentially troublesome time for the Rat, Ox, Hare and Rooster.

Year of the Sheep

In contrast with the Year of the Horse, this year is one of quiet contemplation, nurture and consolidation. It is an auspicious time for the Hare, Dragon, Sheep, Rooster and Pig, but a potentially troublesome time for the Ox, Dragon, Monkey and Dog.

Year of the Monkey

This is a very uncertain time with unpredictability being the key word. Investors should look into diversifying their finances. It is an auspicious time for the Rat, Dragon, Horse, Monkey, Rooster and Dog, but a potentially troublesome time for the Tiger, Hare and Pig.

Year of the Rooster

There will be a general feeling of agitation and some businesses will experience a number of reversals. It is an auspicious time for the Ox, Snake, Sheep, Monkey, Rooster and Pig, but a potentially troublesome time for the Rat, Tiger and Hare.

Year of the Dog

Loyalty in business and the resistance to takeovers are features of this year. It is an auspicious time for the Tiger, Horse, Monkey, Dog and Pig, but a potentially troublesome time for the Dragon and Snake.

Year of the Pig

Business activity during this year may be rather slow. It is a good time to start new long-term ventures. It is also an auspicious time for the Ox, Hare, Sheep, Dog and Pig, but a potentially troublesome time for the Rat, Tiger, Dragon, Snake and Monkey.

NUMEROLOGY — THE POWER OF YOUR BIRTH DATE

A number of systems for numerology evolved from the wisdom of Pythagoras, a sixth-century B.C. Greek philosopher, who believed that the world was built upon the power of numbers. Names, birthdays and starting dates for projects and businesses can, when reduced to a single digit, reveal many characteristics about your prosperity and that of your business.

To understand the power of numbers in your life and business, numerologists usually find out, among other numbers, your birth number. Your birth number influences your life path and indicates what your future may hold concerning your fortune. This can also be applied to your business.

To ascertain your birth number or that of your business, add up all the digits of your birth date and then reduce it down to a single digit number, unless your number adds up to 11, 22 or 33. These three numbers are thought to be "master numbers" and are symbolic of a path aligned with higher spirituality. Do a similar exercise for your business, focusing on the date when your company came into existence — this can be when you conceived the concept, when you legally brought the business into being or when you first started trading.

$$
\begin{aligned}
\textit{For instance, March 27, 1960} &= 2 + 7 + 3 + 1 + 9 + 6 + 0 \\
&= 28 \\
&= 10 \\
&= 1
\end{aligned}
$$

The numbers one to nine were assigned by Pythagoras and others with certain qualities that are outlined in the table below. To find your name number, see page 48.

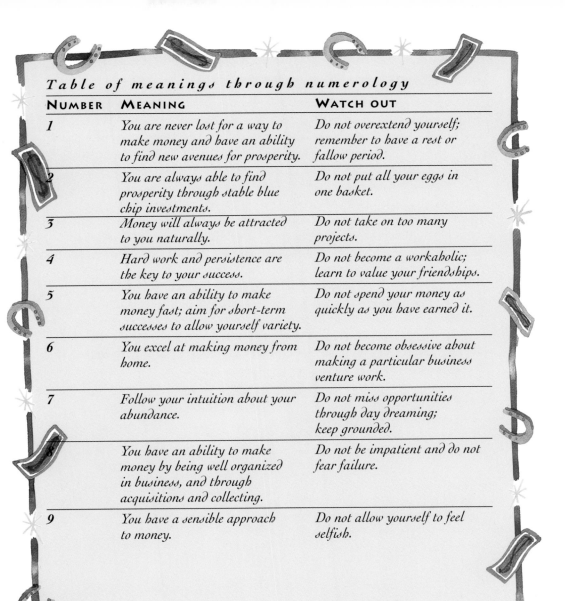

Table of meanings through numerology

NUMBER	MEANING	WATCH OUT
1	You are never lost for a way to make money and have an ability to find new avenues for prosperity.	Do not overextend yourself; remember to have a rest or fallow period.
2	You are always able to find prosperity through stable blue chip investments.	Do not put all your eggs in one basket.
3	Money will always be attracted to you naturally.	Do not take on too many projects.
4	Hard work and persistence are the key to your success.	Do not become a workaholic; learn to value your friendships.
5	You have an ability to make money fast; aim for short-term successes to allow yourself variety.	Do not spend your money as quickly as you have earned it.
6	You excel at making money from home.	Do not become obsessive about making a particular business venture work.
7	Follow your intuition about your abundance.	Do not miss opportunities through day dreaming; keep grounded.
8	You have an ability to make money by being well organized in business, and through acquisitions and collecting.	Do not be impatient and do not fear failure.
9	You have a sensible approach to money.	Do not allow yourself to feel selfish.

TAROT — UNDERSTANDING THE CARDS

The Tarot deck is a form of divination, which is thought by some to have evolved from ancient Egyptian magical texts. The deck comprises 78 cards which are divided into the major arcana of 22 cards and the minor arcana of 56 cards. The minor arcana is divided into four groups, representing the four elements. Particularly linked to money matters, the pentacles or coin suite corresponds with the element of earth.

Each of the minor arcana suites has four court cards and ten numbered cards. The court cards — the King, Queen, Knight and Page — usually represent people, a dominant male, a dominant female, an ambitious person (the knight) and a youngster (the page), while the numbered cards follow a cycle of events from new beginnings to completion.

If you wish to specifically concentrate on your finances, pull out the pentacle suite from the rest of the Tarot pack and, after concentrating on your question about your monetary affairs and handling the cards, pull out one card at random. Use the following table to decide its meaning. You might find that the card you have pulled out is reversed, which means that the picture is upside down. The table below also lists the meanings of reversals. Choosing a time when you will not be disturbed, concentrate on the card. As you focus on it, allow thoughts to come that may provide any further insights on your situation or solutions.

38

Table of the pentacle suite

NUMBER	MEANING OF UPRIGHT POSITION	MEANING OF REVERSED POSITION
King	cautious but talented businessman	man who is mean with money
Queen	supportive businesswoman	woman who is unable to share her good fortune
Knight	excellent administrator	young person who fears risk
Page	young child who indicates small financial gains	young child who indicates petty theft
Ace	financial improvements	loss of finances
2	development of another form of income	unstable sources of money
3	reward for effort	delay in financial reward
4	financial security	feelings of insecurity
5	financial uncertainty	losses will only be temporary
6	help is on its way	careless loss of money or business
7	slow gains	need to change direction
8	further education	feelings of being underrated
9	security and enjoyment of wealth	security endangered
10	money from inheritance, sale of home	anxieties

The Tarot is an excellent way of finding out what issues were involved in your experiencing your particular financial situation and what elements will come into play to help you get out of your problems. If this is the guidance you need, it is best not to segregate the cards but to let them speak to you and put your finances and feelings of abundance in context. It may well be that your financial situation is the result of an emotional unhappiness rather than a straight financial issue.

If you have experienced a feeling of being inadequate and undeserving of prosperity, it is possible that those feelings are the result of parental conditioning. To allow prosperity in your life you may need to focus on these feelings and use your logic to find that there is no real basis for them.

The major arcana represents 22 aspects of the human life. When tailored to money magic purposes, the major arcana cards can be interpreted according to the following:

Table of meanings — the major arcana

CARD NUMBER	NAME	MEANING OF UPRIGHT POSITION	MEANING OF REVERSED POSITION
0	The Fool	new risky venture	gambling on the future
1	The Magician	creative guidance	denial of guidance
2	The High Priestess	secrets (your competitive edge)	concealed or secret enemies
3	The Empress	growth and abundance	lack of money
4	The Emperor	responsibility and leadership	lack of direction
5	The High Priest	education	rebelling against restraints
6	The Lovers	choice between two paths	risky new partnership and possible deception
7	The Chariot	business travel	lack of direction
8	Justice	weighing up the pros and cons	injustice and possible legal wrangles
9	The Hermit	good advice	restlessness

CARD NUMBER	NAME	MEANING OF UPRIGHT POSITION	MEANING OF REVERSED POSITION
10	The Wheel of Fortune	sudden good luck	delays out of your control
11	Strength	determination	doubt
12	The Hanged Man	self-sacrifice	unwillingness to learn
13	Death	transition	stagnation
14	Temperance	teamwork	disagreements
15	The Devil	financial concerns	release from worry
16	The Tower	upheaval	inflexibility
17	The Star	hope	stress
18	The Moon	ungrounded illusion and confusion	check the fine print
19	The Sun	fulfillment and success	exposure of wrong doings
20	Judgment	new ideas	punishment for failure to act
21	The World	completion and success	exhaustion leading to failure to complete project

To use the Tarot, keep a question in mind, and shuffle the cards. Many patterns can be adopted to help read the solution. A simple method to use is the Horseshoe spread, which involves choosing seven cards from your deck and placing them in a horseshoe pattern from left to right (see pattern). You may wish to do this spread using only the major arcana cards, particularly if your question is a serious one.

Experiment with some of the many Tarot decks now available, finding the images that suit you best.

1. The past
2. The present
3. As yet unconsidered influences
4. Obstacles
5. Outside circumstances
6. Best solution
7. Outcome

I CHING — YOUR FORTUNE AT A TOSS OF A COIN

The *I Ching*, or Book of Changes, is a complex, lyrical method of divination that has been simplified over the years to make it widely accessible. It is advised that a more thorough study of the *I Ching* should be attempted if this form of divination appeals to you.

There are sixty-four sections in the *I Ching*, which give guidance for any sort of problem. Each section is symbolized by a hexagram, which is a vertical stack of six broken or unbroken horizontal lines. To access the wisdom of the hexagram appropriate to your question, you must learn how to construct each line, finding out whether each line is broken or unbroken.

One of the simplest ways of consulting the *I Ching* is to throw a coin six times, noting whether it falls heads or tails. If you have thrown heads, this corresponds with yang energy which in turn means an unbroken line. If you have thrown tails, this corresponds with yin energy which in turn means a broken line:

——————— *heads* (yang energy)
—— —— *tails* (yin energy)

Sit in a quiet place, and think of the question concerning your finances with which you wish to consult the *I Ching*, such as: "What should I do to become abundant?" Focus on the coin you wish to use. You may have a lucky coin that you wish to use (either Western or Eastern in origin) for this purpose.

Start at the bottom of your stack and note down whether you have a broken or unbroken line for each of the six levels. You should have something like this:

	(Example)	
(Broken line)	—— ——	*sixth throw*
(Broken line)	—— ——	*fifth throw*
(Broken line)	—— ——	*fourth throw*
(Unbroken line)	————————	*third throw*
(Unbroken line)	————————	*second throw*
(Unbroken line)	—— ——	*first throw*

Each hexagram in the *I Ching* has a number. Consult the table below to find out the number of the hexagram which you have tossed. Look again at your hexagram and note the configuration of the top three lines. Find the match in the upper horizontal line of the table below. Now look at the bottom three lines of your hexagram and find a match in the vertical line. Trace a line down from your top line and across from your side line to find the number of your hexagram. The example on page 42 corresponds with number 46.

HEXAGRAM TABLE

Lower \ Upper								
	1	11	34	5	26	9	14	43
	12	2	16	8	23	20	35	45
	25	24	51	3	27	42	21	17
	6	7	40	29	4	59	64	47
	33	15	62	39	52	53	56	31
	44	46	32	48	18	57	50	28
	13	36	55	63	22	37	30	49
	10	19	54	60	41	61	38	58

Once you have found out the number, consult the table on page 44–45 to understand its advice. Sometimes, it may not be the right time to consult the *I Ching*. Chinese seers would throw two wooden pieces, which were curved on one side and flat on the other to determine whether it was a good time to use the *I Ching*. The two pieces were thrown three times and if, on each throw, both landed with the flat side up, it was best to consult the *I Ching* at another time.

NUMBER AND MEANING

1   Have faith in the plans you have already made.
2   Do not force the issue and wait for the right time.
3   Allow the issue to germinate further.
4   Great future promised but be patient now.
5   Great success but you will need to bide your time and not force the issue.
6   Take the advice of an experienced person.
7   You may be in line for a promotion.
8   A partnership will instinctively evolve and will be successful.
9   You will initially receive small gains until you feel sincere about your actions.
10   Plan any bold moves with caution.
11   Do not force an issue but approach it sensitively and have a clear mind.
12   There are some obstacles which can be averted with firmness and patience.
13   Teamwork will be successful if there is true unity.
14   You will receive great insight and true wisdom.
15   You may have to show humility before succeeding in a big enterprise.
16   Seek a balance and do not reach for easy gratification.
17   There are no obstacles to your plans and you are able to proceed easily.
18   Avoid compulsive behavior and find your inner balance.
19   Although the situation runs smoothly right now, take care of the future.
20   Take the time to contemplate your actions.
21   You may need to engage in some legal action to continue success.
22   You will need to resolve the bigger issue.
23   Do not make any changes yet but examine the past to transform your fears into strengths.
24   Correct a small mistake and continue on your path.
25   Watch out for unexpected events.
26   Help others with your own wealth and wisdom.
27   Look after your health and try to alleviate stress so that your actions are not undermined.
28   Your plan of action is excellent but needs firmer foundations.
29   You must stay in your situation and wait until a way out shows itself.
30   Learn to be tolerant and compliant and you will find your place in the world.
31   Be flexible and open to change.
32   Do not make any changes.
33   Take time to be alone and seek insight from the past about your ambitions.
34   Your plans will be very successful if you are disciplined.

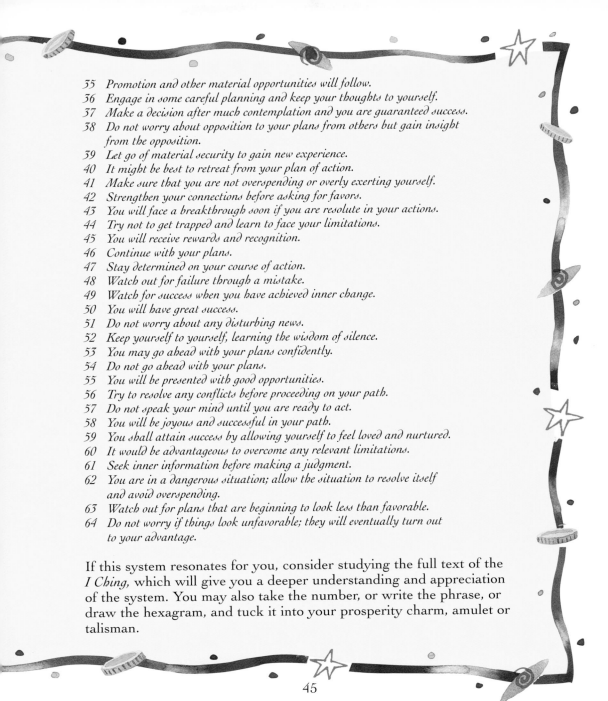

35   Promotion and other material opportunities will follow.
36   Engage in some careful planning and keep your thoughts to yourself.
37   Make a decision after much contemplation and you are guaranteed success.
38   Do not worry about opposition to your plans from others but gain insight from the opposition.
39   Let go of material security to gain new experience.
40   It might be best to retreat from your plan of action.
41   Make sure that you are not overspending or overly exerting yourself.
42   Strengthen your connections before asking for favors.
43   You will face a breakthrough soon if you are resolute in your actions.
44   Try not to get trapped and learn to face your limitations.
45   You will receive rewards and recognition.
46   Continue with your plans.
47   Stay determined on your course of action.
48   Watch out for failure through a mistake.
49   Watch for success when you have achieved inner change.
50   You will have great success.
51   Do not worry about any disturbing news.
52   Keep yourself to yourself, learning the wisdom of silence.
53   You may go ahead with your plans confidently.
54   Do not go ahead with your plans.
55   You will be presented with good opportunities.
56   Try to resolve any conflicts before proceeding on your path.
57   Do not speak your mind until you are ready to act.
58   You will be joyous and successful in your path.
59   You shall attain success by allowing yourself to feel loved and nurtured.
60   It would be advantageous to overcome any relevant limitations.
61   Seek inner information before making a judgment.
62   You are in a dangerous situation; allow the situation to resolve itself and avoid overspending.
63   Watch out for plans that are beginning to look less than favorable.
64   Do not worry if things look unfavorable; they will eventually turn out to your advantage.

If this system resonates for you, consider studying the full text of the *I Ching*, which will give you a deeper understanding and appreciation of the system. You may also take the number, or write the phrase, or draw the hexagram, and tuck it into your prosperity charm, amulet or talisman.

FEELING LUCKY — MAGICALLY

GOOD LUCK CHARMS FROM ANCIENT TIMES

Lucky charms are often traditional words, chants or prayers that have been used through the ages to attract all kinds of desirable outcomes, such as a new loved one or a hefty fortune.

The power of charms is well known in folklore. A collection of charms and verses have been handed down, the source often obscured over many centuries and the original words sometimes varied, misspelled, altered or replaced. However, often the intent and use of those words over generations for a particular purpose have imbued even nonsensical words with power.

Charms can be a single word or phrase that can be spoken or written down on paper, parchment, wood or even engraved upon a metal object. It can be as simple as one word that encapsulates what you want, such as "wealth" or even something as commonplace as "washing machine".

If spoken, it is important that you put as much feeling into the uttering of the word or phrase. You may wish to experiment with this by saying your special word when you receive your pay, particularly if you are paid on a Thursday. Thursdays are particularly lucky for money matters. Each week, perhaps when you receive your pay statement, look at the amount and say your special word or phrase and visualize the amount of your pay tripled or with an extra zero at the end.

If written on an object, a charm can be carried around with you, as long as you wrap it up in its own linen, cotton or leather bag or pouch. If you are waiting for news of a promotion at work, consider placing your charm, discretely packaged in its bag or pouch, on your desk in the top left-hand corner — your wealth sector in feng shui.

There are a number of traditional good-luck charms, which should really be called lucky amulets or talismans, such as the horseshoe. The horseshoe, thought to represent the new or crescent moon, is believed to be lucky if it is worn or displayed with its points up, so as to contain the good luck that falls into the "U" shape.

Charms can also be natural objects, such as dried bayberries or the bayberry bark. Bayberries, as well as cedar, are reputed to attract money. Keep some of the berries, the bark or the cedar in your wallet or purse. Certain gems and crystals are believed to be lucky, such as the moonstone, particularly if it is bathed with the light of the new moon as you charge it with your wish for luck.

ANCIENT WISDOM

Assume that everything that happens to you does so for some good. That if you decided to be lucky, you are lucky. All events contain an advantage for you — if you look for it! Epictetus, The Art of Living (55 A.D.-135 A.D.)

LUCKY NUMBERS

Essentially, your lucky numbers are those about which you have some good feeling. They can be any number that reminds you of something that happened to you in life. Or you may notice that a particular number, or numbers, often crops up in your life.

In numerology, it is generally thought that even numbers such as 2, 4, 6 and 8 represent stability, while odd numbers represent creativity. In ancient Chinese beliefs, odd numbers were thought to be unlucky, except the number 5. Also, your lucky number could be your numerological birth number (see pages 36–37) or your name number.

To ascertain your name number, assign a number for each letter in your name by using the following table:

1	2	3	4	5	6	7	8	9
A	B	C	D	E	F	G	H	I
J	K	L	M	N	O	P	Q	R
S	T	U	V	W	X	Y	Z	

For instance, Antonia Beattie $= 1 + 5 + 2 + 6 + 5 + 9 + 1 + 2 + 5 + 1 + 2 + 2 + 9 + 5$
$$= 55$$
$$= 1 \; (\textit{Two numbers added together to get single digit})$$

In ancient Chinese numerology, certain numbers are believed to bring good or bad luck. It is important to remember that for various cultures, different numbers are lucky or unlucky because they signify certain cultural beliefs.

For example, the number 4 is believed by the Chinese to be bad luck, auguring death, while 5 is thought to be a lucky number because it symbolizes the five elements — earth, water, fire, wood and metal — which are the basis of Chinese medicine and religious beliefs. However, the basis of many Western mystical traditions are the four elements — earth, air, fire and water. Consequently, the number 4 is believed to be a lucky number in the West.

It is important to assess your own feelings about particular numbers. Jot down in your journal or daily diary, numbers that have been lucky for you. You may see patterns that you can use to predict your own good fortune.

ANIMAL IMAGES

According to Native North American beliefs, the shaman is able to make a powerful connection with the wisdom of the spirit world by linking into three levels of spirit guides. The upper astral world consists of teacher guides, while the middle astral world is inhabited by the recently dead or concerned ancestors. The lower plane consists of "power animals".

The shaman is often associated with birds, and some wear masks to connect with such power animals as the eagle, hawk, owl or raven.

You too can connect with your own power animal depending on what characteristics you wish to borrow to enhance your financial situation. If you are going into a tricky business deal that will need a great deal of cunning and strategy, you may wish to invoke the power of the fox. If you wish for a well-appointed home, you may seek the power of the rabbit.

To invoke the spirit of an animal, meditate on your current financial needs and open your mind to any animal images that would be helpful for the successful outcome of your project, strategy or wishes. Sometimes, you will not see an animal in your meditation, but do not be surprised if a creature runs across your path soon afterward. Read up on the animal's characteristics and use the most appropriate ones in your business dealings.

SYMBOLIC ANIMALS
Bear: *protection*
Eagle: *better communication*
Frog: *happiness*
Hawk: *clear vision and prophesy*
Horse: *prosperity*
Rabbit: *peace*

MAKING YOUR OWN GOOD LUCK CHARM

To make an effective good-luck charm, you will need a powerful word, something to write it on and something to contain the magic of the written charm. You may also wish to include in your lucky charm package an herbal amulet, a favorite stone, a lucky coin and/or an image of an animal whose characteristics you wish to harness for luck.

Consider making your charm during a time ruled by the influence of Jupiter, a planet that is said to have a great effect on our fortunes. A particularly potent time for money magic is the third hour after sunset on a Thursday evening. If a Thursday coincides with a new moon, make sure to take advantage of this time.

Gather all the pieces that you want to include in your lucky charm in a place where you will not be disturbed. Also bring with you a special or favorite pen and two lengths of green ribbon or string. Have in your mind your word or phrase that sums up all aspects of what luck means to you. You may simply choose to use the word "luck" or "$50,000".

Set out the pieces of your charm on a table, the floor or any other place where you would feel comfortable to do the work. It is preferable if the moon can be seen from where you are sitting, especially if it is shedding some light over your pieces.

When you are comfortable, write your special word or phrase on a small piece of parchment or parchment-like paper with your special pen or on a piece of wood, preferably a sliver or small chunk of cedar. As you are making this charm, say repeatedly under your breath or aloud, the word or phrase you have written.

Still repeating the charm, roll up the paper into a small coil and tie it with your green thread or ribbon. If you have used wood, go to the next stage of the charm and place the wood or paper in a simple bag of cloth, preferably of a green-dyed natural fabric. Include your other items. You may wish to insert some lavender, a stabilizing herb, or a stone that resonates to the energy of Jupiter, such as blue sapphire, amethyst, turquoise or carnelian. If you are entering into a risky venture or are having a flutter at the races, include a piece of green-colored aventurine.

Once you have included all the pieces you wish your lucky charm to hold, close the bag and tie it with the rest of your green ribbon. With a final intake of breath, imagine that you are breathing strong energy from the moon down into your hands. Feel your hands vibrate with power and allow that power to be transferred into the green lucky charm. Exhale and feel that the energy has been imbedded into your charm.

Once you have closed your bag, it is important to never open it again. Tie a knot in the string and, if the string has a tendency to slip, drip some wax from a green candle on the knot.

To enhance the power of your lucky charm package, consecrate it to the four elements. To consecrate means to dedicate the purpose of the object to your desire. You can do this by sprinkling the charm with salted water (water), passing it quickly over a flame (fire) and incense smoke (air) and then sprinkling earth or salt over it (earth).

Be sure to also look at making an amulet protecting you from bad luck (see pages 72–73).

Some stones, such as amethyst, turquoise and garnet, are said to lose their brightness and/or color when their owner is about to experience disaster, such as a financial downturn.

ATTRACTING PROSPERITY AND ABUNDANCE

MAGICAL ETHICS

The spells, charms and other techniques in money magic are beneficial in nature and must be worked without feelings of selfishness and greed (see page 14). It is important to remember the traditional law of Western magic: "If it harms none, do what you will."

First you must attune your will so that your actions do not harm anyone and so that you are acting in harmony with your true goal in life. Seek to feel abundance by incorporating actions that are those of an abundant person. Consider sharing any good fortune you gain through money magic and spreading a sense of prosperity to those around you.

If you are suffering from harmful competition in your business, think wisely what spell you should cast. Do not do anything that will harm or "bind" your competitor. Binding is a spell in which you literally bind an image of your competitor with black cord. The danger in such practices are akin to the Eastern concept of karma, that whatever is sent out returns in time upon the sender. In Western magic, the formula is said to be "that which is sent out returns threefold."

Sometimes it is legitimate to work a spell that will bind someone from doing harm to others. White witches have been known to work such magic when it is perceived to be for the greater good. However, there is always a price to be paid.

As you have seen, to achieve a successful result through your spellcraft it is important to focus clearly on the outcome you want. But you also need to give yourself the time to think through the consequences of the spell.

MIRROR MAGIC

Mirror magic is a very simple yet powerful way of attracting abundance
to you. All you need is a full-length mirror, which you can set up in
a place where you will not be disturbed, and allow yourself at least
an hour to fully relax into the exercise.

You may appear before your mirror in one of two ways. If your
issues concerning money magic revolve around attracting abundance
from your employer or through gaining the right contacts, prepare
for this exercise by putting on your most flattering, favorite or
powerful business clothes. If you have a "lucky" scarf, pair of socks
or some other "lucky" garment, include that in your money magic outfit.

If your issue with money magic is to increase your feeling that you
can and will control your fortunes and make your own money,
consider doing this exercise naked.

Before doing this exercise, take a bath or shower to cleanse the stress
of the day away. When ready, anoint your heart and your forehead with
a drop of lavender oil and light two green candles on either side of your
mirror. Stand in front of the mirror, becoming aware of the sensations
of your body. Check particularly how your back feels. If your lower
back feels a little strain while standing, tilt your pelvis forward and
slightly bend your knees.

Look at yourself in the mirror. Try to distance yourself from your old
reactions of yourself by concentrating on your breathing. Move on to feel
the energy in your feet sinking through the floor down into the earth.
You may begin to feel a sense of increased stability.

Allow a feeling of abundance to wash over you. What does abundance
mean to you? It might include a sense of being supported or of having
absolute freedom to do whatever you want. Imagine those feelings within
you as if you have already achieved them and allow your clothing or
body to be saturated with those feelings. Feel a strong glow encompass
your whole body. Work on this image for three consecutive nights before
the mirror and see if people begin to treat you any differently.

SPELLS

To make a spell work you must first decide what you want. Second, you must concentrate on what you want with the firm belief that you will get it (see page 52 about the ethics of magic). Such concentration helps you open an "astral doorway" to a new reality in which your goal has already been achieved. Once you have "keyed" it in on the astral plane, your wish will soon filter down into the everyday world.

Many spells are devised so that you collect specific images and objects or say words that help your concentration, such as using green candles for a money spell.

SPELL TO ATTRACT ABUNDANCE AND PROSPERITY

Tools required

- *Green/blue non-drip candle*
- *One drop of cedarwood or lavender essential oil, with a few sprigs of lavender if you wish.*
- *Wheel of Fortune card from a Tarot deck*

Timing and symbol

Day: Thursday
Symbol for Jupiter:

This spell should be cast during the waxing of the moon on a Thursday in the third hour after sunset. Inscribe the appropriate planetary image on your candle and sprinkle it with your oil and lavender sprigs or lavender essential oil. Light the candle. Focus on the candlelight and visualize what you want to achieve by this spell. For instance, money to buy a new car. Take the Tarot card and focus on the image bathed by the candlelight and say the following words nine times:

May this spell work for the benefit of all concerned.

You may choose another card from the Tarot deck that you believe will better symbolize your wish in relation to your financial circumstances (see pages 38–41).

Depending on how practiced you are, sit focusing on the image until you feel you have put enough energy into the spell. Place the candle in a bowl of sand and stand it in a tiled area of your home. If you put it in the bath tub or sink, make sure that a plug is covering the hole. Put the Tarot card on your desk or dressing table, on the top left-hand side corner, for three days and nights.

SPELL TO ATTRACT NEW ENERGY

Another type of spell is a cleansing spell which attracts new energy by cleaning out old energy. Empty your wallet or purse of every bit of money, plastic and paper, and clean it of any stray particles of dirt or lint. If it is made of leather, give your wallet or purse a bit of a polish.

Put your money, credit cards and identification back into the wallet, making sure that everything is in order; arrange your bank notes in order of currency value and sort your coins into silver, gold or bronze. Also include a thin sliver of cedar with your wallet or purse. Apart from discouraging moths, cedarwood will attract money to you.

This is an ongoing spell, so after a week, see that your wallet is still as organized and clean as when you first started. As you continue doing this once a week (preferably on a Thursday), you should find that opportunities for making money begin to emerge and that you are feeling more organized about money matters.

Some stones have the ability to have a magnetic attraction concerning money. In particular, catch the flash of red in a small piece of fire opal in the light of a green candle while visualizing an increase in the number of customers or clients. Place the charged stone near your phone or in your shop to attract customers to your outlet or service.

TALISMANS

A talisman is any object that makes the wearer feel powerful. Some say that the most famous talisman is the mythic Philosopher's Stone, which can allegedly give an alchemist the power to turn base metals into gold. Unlike amulets, which passively protect their wearers, talismans contain supernatural powers which give special powers to the wearer, such as the power to make fortunes.

It is thought that the certain sigils, numbers or words used on talismans set up a delicate vibration that help the wearer attain these special powers. Sigils include a design or image intended to symbolize a deity or a magical concept and they serve as a focus for calling upon that deity or spirit.

The Kabbalists used numbers in magical squares to create powerful talismans. The magic of such a square is that the numbers are arranged so that they add up, either horizontally or vertically, to the same answer.

Kabbalists used seven magical squares which were linked to the five planets visible to the naked eye, as well as the sun and moon. The one for Jupiter is known to have effective powers over the gathering of prosperity, prestige and honor.

Talismans can be made from any type of material. For money magic, a talisman can be shaped out of a small piece of silver or tin. If you are familiar with engraving silver, you may be able to wear a talisman upon which the Square of Jupiter is engraved. If you use tin (a metal of Jupiter) as the base for the Square, you may wish to wear it in a protective pouch or silver locket.

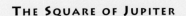

4	14	15	1
9	7	6	12
5	11	10	8
16	2	3	13

A sigil may be made by linking up the numbers in the square with those that numerological correspond with letters of your name (see page 48). For instance:

A N T O N I A = 1 + 5 + 2 + 6 + 5 + 9 + 1
will make the following shape:

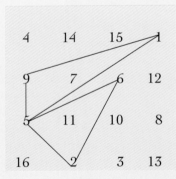

By making a sigil of your name using the Jupiter Square, you are linking into the expansive power of Jupiter to grant you success and prosperity.

DREAM MAGIC

Current Western thinking says that dreams are the world of your unconscious mind. When dreaming, the unconscious mind has access to all your fears, desires and inhibitions, and randomly weaves inner visions that show you pictures, sounds, feelings and scents.

Some of the symbols used are common to all who dream as they tap into the collective unconscious, a vast collection of knowledge that can be accessed by everyone. Other symbols are specifically geared to the individual who dreams it.

To understand your dreams, buy a journal of a generous size and keep a record of the dreams you have, particularly if you are experiencing an unsettling or a financially challenging time. After a week, reread your entries and see if a consistent theme is emerging. In this way, you can start to learn from your dreams.

Other forms of dream magic are best practiced during a full moon. If you seek information about a new business venture or a project that might be financially rewarding, you can use the light of the full moon to cleanse your pillows of any previous negative energies before you dedicate your night's dreaming to your purpose. Air your pillows and fluff them in the light of the full moon.

Write down your question for your unconscious. Allow yourself to focus on your purpose. Leaving your journal open, go to sleep. When you awake, perhaps during the night, write down your dream, even if it does not immediately seem to be pertinent to your financial issues. Take your journal with you during the day and allow your mind at times to refocus on the dream you remembered and the words you have used to record it. Continue to jot down impressions about the message of the dream during the day. Repeat this over three consecutive nights and see if a common thread or solution is emerging.

PREVENTING NIGHTMARES

It is believed that dreams give us important information about ourselves, some of which may be quite disturbing, even when they are giving us beneficial insights. If you suffer from nightmares, a traditional cure is to place a sprig of rosemary or thyme under your pillow.

You may also consider purchasing or making a dreamcatcher. According to Native American beliefs, dreams are communications from the spirits. However, some spirits are thought to be evil and dreamcatchers were designed to hang over a person's bed to trap their dreams in the web, allowing only the beneficial dreams to glide down a beaded and feathered string into sleeper's head.

MAKING YOUR HOME AND OFFICE PROSPEROUS

ENHANCING GOOD LUCK IN YOUR HOME AND OFFICE

To create good luck in your home and office there are a number of wealth symbols that can be auspiciously placed to attract wealth, luck and longevity. In feng shui, gold and both artificial and naturally occurring gold-colored objects, such as brass coins, oranges and pineapples, are always considered symbols of good luck.

In ancient Chinese beliefs, there are three types of luck. They are fate, as well as the luck that you create for yourself and earth luck. Earth luck occurs when you are attuned with the energy of the earth, either through your own intuition or by the study of feng shui. In Western magic, it is also believed that by strengthening your intuition and learning to tap into the energy of the earth by "grounding", a person can attain this form of good luck, which will help them mitigate even the worst of fates.

Placement of good luck or wealth symbols in the home is important. Never place such symbols on the floor or in a low position. Find an elevated location, such as a mantelpiece, above the door or even on the coffee table.

In decorating your wealth sector (see page 62), you must keep in mind that this area resonates to the Chinese element of wood and should influence the color schemes and objects you use to decorate this sector of the house. Colors such as light greens and shades of brown and tan will enhance the wealth energy in your home,

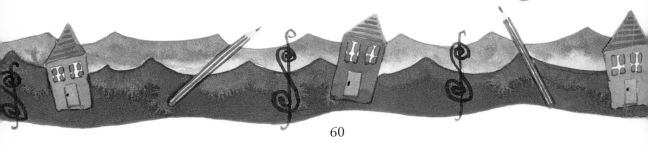

as will the incorporation of a number of potted plants. One simple way to increase your wealth is to place under a potted plant three gold-colored coins that have been wrapped in red paper.

In Chinese beliefs, the five elements have a particular interaction with each other, which can be either productive or destructive. Some elements, such as water and wood, react well together because water is said to create wood whereas metal is thought to be harmful to wood.

When decorating your wealth area in your house, do not use much metal but concentrate on both water and wood motifs. You may even consider installing an aquarium with nine fish, preferably eight goldfish and one black fish. The role of the black fish is to symbolically gobble up any bad wealth energy that may stray into your home.

If you have built a new house or are repaving your driveway, consider burying nine coins in your driveway before you pour the cement or gravel, or begin paving. Bury the coins along an imaginary line that leads to your door, and this will help attract abundant wealth energy to your door. Alternatively, place nine coins under your welcome mat.

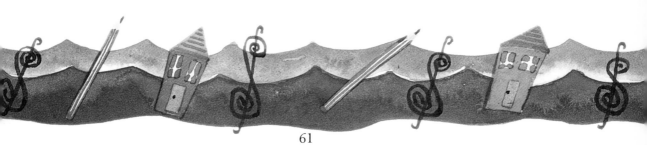

CORRECTING THE FLOW OF ENERGY IN YOUR HOME

In a simple form of feng shui, the area of your home, which is believed to correlate with your level of wealth, is in the back left-hand corner of your home as you stand looking inside your house from your front door.

It is believed that if your house is irregularly shaped and that particular corner is missing, you will continuously have problems with your finances. The trick is to square off that portion of the house to try and make it appear to have a regular shape. To square off, continue the lines of your outside walls and find the point in the garden where they meet. Feng shui practitioners often advise placing a water feature, such as a fountain, to strengthen the corner made by the meeting of these imaginary walls. You may wish to highlight the wealth-enhancing factor of that corner by constructing a kidney-shaped pond to contain a few goldfish or, if the pond is large enough, some carp.

If your wealth corner contains a water feature in the house, such as a bathroom, toilet, kitchen or laundry, be careful that you are not flushing away your wealth energy. Wealth is particularly linked with yin energy and the element of water. It follows that all areas in your home dealing with water, such as sinks, bath and laundry tubs and toilets, must be in good working order and not blocked in any way. So that you are not losing your wealth, it is important to do the following things:

- fix leaky taps immediately;
- always flush your toilet with the lid down;
- cover all floor drain holes; and
- keep the laundry and bathroom doors closed at all times.

Feng shui gives us a number of simple and practical solutions for poor flows of energy through your home. According to the principles of feng shui, positive energy (sheng qi) can be encouraged along gently curving lines while negative energy (sha qi) flows in straight lines.

It is important that the universal energy (qi) is encouraged to flow through your house slowly, without obstructions, bringing with it good luck, prosperity and well-being. If the energy becomes obstructed or is encouraged to move in straight lines, the energy can become stagnant or destructive. For example, if your front and back doors are facing each other, this encourages the beneficial or lucky energy to flow quickly right through your house. A popular cure is to hang a crystal or a set of wind chimes just inside the front door to slow down the energy and allow it to bring good luck to your home.

CLEARING YOUR DESK

If you work at a desk, apply some feng shui to increase your sense of wealth and good fortune. The first step is to move your desk into an auspicious position, positioned so that you are facing the wall which frames the doorway leading into your office. However, often you are not able to move your office furniture to allow for feng shui. If this is so, and your back is facing the entrance to your office, you may "cure" this bad flow of energy by placing a mirror on your desk so that the entrance is reflected in it.

Good luck and fortune can be encouraged by the state of your desk. Above all else, your desk must be absolutely clear of clutter. Remove all objects that are not in everyday use and keep your desk drawers tidy and functional. This in itself will attract good feng shui.

The second step is to identify the wealth sector in your office. As at home, your wealth sector is in the far left-hand corner as you are facing your office from the door. See if you can place a healthy plant in that section of the room, not forgetting to put a coin under the base of the pot or at the base of the plant rising out of the potted soil.

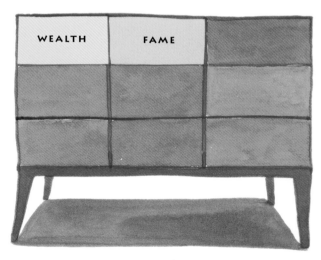

The third step is to identify the wealth sector of your desk. Sit facing your desk and mentally divide it into the following nine sections.

The top third section of your desk on your left-hand side corresponds with the wealth area in your home. The next third section along the top of your desk is considered to correspond with fame and acknowledgement. To encourage good fortune in these areas, place there a picture of vividly colored flowers or a package of three coins wrapped in red paper or tied up with red ribbon or thread. Depending on your aesthetic, you may wish to instead place a small artificial jade tree or some brightly colored silk or wooden carved flowers.

You may also decorate these two areas of your desk with a vase of very fresh flowers. The energy of flowers is short-lived and they must be replaced immediately the moment they start to droop. You do not want dying energy in your wealth, or any other, sector. Similarly, it is ill-advised to place dried flowers on your desk.

Use fresh flowers on your desk only for a special occasion, such as when you are waiting for a promotion (which also involves a salary increase) or if you are waiting for a contract to come through. Remember to tie a red ribbon around the vase and to place a small gold or silver coin under the base of the vase.

Feng shui practitioners also advise against placing plants that are stunted in their growth or that are prickly to touch. So avoid placing on the wealth sector of your desk plants such as bonsai trees or shrubs, roses or cacti.

SPECIAL TIPS FOR YOUR BUSINESS

There are a number of ways to increase your profits if you work in, or own, a retail outlet. First, examine the areas where money exchanges hands. Is your sales desk cluttered or well organized? Does your sales desk face the street door? Where does your cash register sit? Where is your telephone placed?

Divide your sales desk into the following feng shui segments:

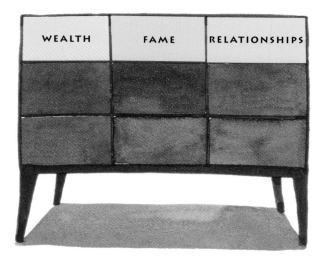

Experiment with placing your cash register in the wealth sector and your telephone in the relationships sector, particularly if you have customers contacting you to make over-the-phone purchases or if you are in a business in which customers tend to contact you in response to advertising.

Try this for a week. You may wish to experiment further by sticking a coin tied with red thread, string, ribbon or tape onto your cash register and telephone handle. You may also consider placing a small mirror behind the cash register to reflect and symbolically double your takings.

If practicable, also place plants in the wealth sector (back left-hand corner) on the shop floor and incorporate a simple water feature near the plants. This can take the shape of a glass bowl, which has a simple fish tank pump that circulates water around some naturalistically arranged pebbles, semi-precious stones (such as quartz crystals or amethysts) and incorporating a water-loving plant.

According to Chinese beliefs, both numbers eight and nine are auspicious to business. Eight is believed to be a number auspicious for growth and stability in business. Nine is a particularly auspicious business number and has been considered a magical number for many centuries because no matter how you multiply the number you always end up with nine when the digits of the answer to the multiplication are added up, for example:

$$27 \times 9 = 243$$
$$2 + 4 + 3 = 9$$

THE SIGNIFICANCE OF NUMBERS ACCORDING TO CHINESE BELIEFS

1 - bad luck
2 - effortless fulfillment
3 - bad luck
4 - bad luck, particularly for endings
5 - good luck
6 - the acquisition of wealth
7 - good luck
8 - the prospect of wealth
9 - longevity
10 - sureness

Take your local business telephone number and add up all the digits. What number do you come up with? Add up your local business telephone number with your area code if you do business with interstate customers, then do the same exercise using your country, area and local number if you do business with overseas customers.

PROTECTING YOURSELF FROM BAD LUCK

SUPERSTITIONS

Over the centuries a number of superstitions or beliefs evolved regarding the various supposed indicators of bad luck. Each country had its own set of superstitions that regulated people's lives. There is one school of thought that believes superstitions have derived their power from centuries of people believing in their power. Gradually over time, the fact that a black cat crosses your path is enough to trigger the expectation of bad luck. However, black cats are not within themselves unlucky, which is evidenced by the fact that certain European cultures considered them to be omens of good fortune.

The same situation occurs about the number 13. Believed by many Western cultures to be unlucky, the number is thought to be a magical number of great power by those of both the Hindu and Jewish faiths. Nevertheless, in the West, the naming of the thirteenth floor in a office block or having thirteen guests to dinner is cause for consternation and effort is usually made to avoid such situations arising. Roman society believed that an odd number of guests created "sinister silences". In late nineteenth-century Paris, a special club developed where men were contacted by frantic hostesses to make a fourteenth at a dinner when one of the guests could not attend at the last moment.

If you or your ancestors have moved away from your original homeland and you do not feel particularly drawn to certain regional superstitions, it might be an idea to investigate the origins of these customs before believing one way or another. However, some superstitions appear to be quite universal or to have common themes, such as the throwing of coins in a body of water.

In both Celtic and other ancient cultures, such as the Aztecs and Mayans, spirits were thought to dwell at the bottom of wells and live near springs and quiet waterways. Human sacrifices were originally made to these spirits to ensure prosperity for the village. Fortunately, over time, humans came to be replaced by coins. It is interesting that in Chinese wisdom, the element of water is believed to be very helpful to prosperity.

Tiger's eye is a stone that is reputed to have the ability to protect its owner from financial ruin. Carry a piece of tiger's eye in your purse and wallet, preferably with your paper money, tucked in closest to the highest denomination.

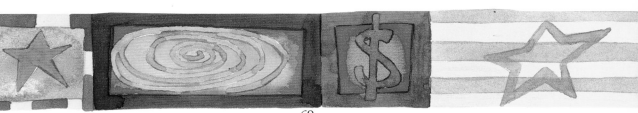

PROTECTION SPELLS

Protection spells against bad luck can be most effective as long as they are based on a strong belief in the power of the spell.

Find a special space where you can be free from distractions for at least an hour. If you are seeking to guard yourself from hardship or discomfort concerning money, such as losing your job or being robbed, scan the herbs, stones and symbols in the table opposite and choose one that calls to you. If none do, concentrate on your purpose and see if another symbol, stone or herb comes to mind.

Place the object in front of you and concentrate on an image of yourself being successful and comfortably secure or of yourself walking down a dark alley without being molested. If you have chosen a stone, hold it in your hand while you visualize the images of success or safety. If you have chosen an image, draw it on a piece of paper or transcribe the image onto fabric or metal, or if you have chosen an herb, place a small amount in a little bag. Hold these while you are imagining the success of your spell. You may wish to chant the following:

> *Let be me*
> *Most safely be*

By holding your herb, stone or symbol, you are charging the objects with the positive outcome or success of your wish. Carry your object with you whenever you feel the need for protection or place it in your cash register.

If you wish to guard your home from being burgled, again focus on the herbs, stones and symbols below and choose two objects that resonate to your home's protection. Follow the steps above and when you have finished your visualization, place one object near your front door and the other near your back door (see also page 74).

The following table of objects lists a selection that would be suitable for use in a spell or an amulet for financial success or for protection against financial worries.

HERBS	STONES	SYMBOLS
Cinnamon sticks	Bloodstone	Jupiter magic square (see page 57)
Cardamom seeds	Tiger's eye	Pentagram (5-pointed star)
Cloves (whole)	Amethyst	Hexagram (6-pointed star)
Nutmeg (whole)	Jade	Octagram (8-pointed star)
Ginger (a dried slice)	Carnelian	Runic symbol for wealth ᚸ
Rosemary	Quartz crystal	Runic symbol for pleasure ᚹ
Bay leaves	Aventurine	Image of a horse
Basil leaves	Garnet	Image of a tiger
Dill seeds	Hematite	Image of a wheel
Juniper berries (whole)	Topaz	Image of a crescent moon

CLEANSING SPELL

To cleanse any bad money energy from your wallet, light a stick of lavender incense or burn a drop or two of lavender essential oil and pass the wallet over the smoke. Lavender is a powerful magical herb for stabilizing energy and is noted for its ability to attract both money and possessions.

MAKING YOUR OWN AMULET OF PROTECTION

At one time, any new business venture which commenced during the full moon was thought to be unlucky, possibly because during the night of the full moon, psychic energy tends to be unstable. Whenever the energy is unstable, it is easier to impose your magical will, so the full moon is an excellent time to focus on magical workings.

Full moon is the time for most workings that involve healing, divination and the making of amulets and talismans for the purpose of, for instance, emotional protection of yourself or others.

An amulet is a protective device which is usually worn on the body. It can take the form of a symbol, such as a magic square (see pages 56–57), a cross or a pentagram, or a pouch that contains herbs, stones or other substances (see pages 70–71).

If two or more objects are put together to form an amulet, they are often incorporated into a locket or a leather or fabric pouch so that they can be carried or worn easily. A small bag can be made out of a circle of leather or silk with a leather thong or silk ribbon threaded evenly through the circumference. Knot the ends of the thong and pull the circle into a small bag within which you can pop a muslin bag containing the appropriate herb or mix of herbs, a symbol and/or a particular stone.

If you are handy with the needle, you may consider embroidering or cross-stitching a hex symbol on your small pouch. While hexing is popularly thought to have connotations of curses and negative magic, hex symbols are, in fact, used for blessings and protection spells. Use a green thread to stitch one of each of the following:

- pentagram, a five-pointed star, for good luck
- hexagram, a six-pointed star, for protection
- octagram, an eight-pointed star, for abundance

If you wish to incorporate a number of items, choose no more than three. To make your own amulet, first think of a specific financial circumstance from which you seek protection. With this thought in mind, scan the table on page 71 and choose the objects that strike you as having protective energies for your situation. Allow your intuition to guide your judgment.

If you are using herbs that you have grown yourself, cut them on a dry day and hang them with string from the ceiling. Traditionally, your herbs should be cut during waxing and full moon for protection against poverty and hardship.

Certain herbs are particularly effective when made up as amulets. Saint John's Wort, which is gathered at summer solstice, is an excellent herb for all-purpose protection.

SPELLCRAFT TIP

When you have finished making your amulet, sprinkle some chamomile into the amulet as the herb is renowned for its promise of success.

SECURING YOUR HOME FROM MISFORTUNE

Doing a blessing for a house or place of business is one way of securing the premises from misfortune. First, you need to cleanse the premises of any negative energies that have stayed within the building. These energies may be sensed if you get a feeling of being, at the very least, slightly uncomfortable in the building or in some part of it. Use your intuition. You may wish to visualize a blue mist attracting all the negative energy to it as it passes through the building. If you do so, allow the mist to finally dissolve into the ground.

Second, set up a protective energy around the house by walking slowly around the outside of the building in a clockwise motion and splash salted water onto the ground. Enter the house and light a white candle at the entrance. The sign of your protective symbol, such as the Cross or a pentagram, should also be made at the main entrance door. In each room make the sign of your protective symbol at the door and windows. If appropriate, take with you a basket which contains the protective amulets that you have prepared previously (see pages 72–73) and place one above each door and window that you feel needs securing. To make sure that the magic holds good, you could also plant basil or dill in a window box to help stabilize the feeling of protection.

TABLE OF CHINESE ASTROLOGY CYCLES —
WHICH ANIMAL ARE YOU?

The table below outlines the years that correspond to a particular animal. By knowing which animal resonates with your birthday, you can see which years will be beneficial to you (see pages 32–35) and you may further wish to work with the image of the animal for good luck charms (pages 50–51) or amulets of protection (see pages 72–73).

RAT

February 5, 1924 — January 24, 1925

January 24, 1936 — February 10, 1937

February 10, 1948 — January 28, 1949

January 28, 1960 — February 14, 1961

February 15, 1972 — February 2, 1973

February 2, 1984 — February 19, 1985

February 19, 1996 — February 6, 1997

OX

January 25, 1925 — February 12, 1926

February 11, 1937 — January 30, 1938

January 29, 1949 — February 16, 1950

February 15, 1961 — February 4, 1962

February 3, 1973 — January 22, 1974

February 20, 1985 — February 8, 1986

February 7, 1997 — January 27, 1998

TIGER

February 13, 1926 — February 1, 1927

January 31, 1938 — February 18, 1939

February 17, 1950 — February 5, 1951

February 5, 1962 — January 24, 1963

January 23, 1974 — February 10, 1975

February 9, 1986 — January 28, 1987

January 28, 1998 — February 15, 1999

HARE

February 2, 1927 — January 22, 1928

February 19, 1939 — February 7, 1940

February 6, 1951 — January 26, 1952

January 25, 1963 — February 12, 1964

February 11, 1975 — January 30, 1976

January 29, 1987 — February 16, 1988

February 16, 1999 — February 4, 2000

TABLE OF CHINESE ASTROLOGY CYCLES —
WHICH ANIMAL ARE YOU?

DRAGON

January 23, 1928 — February 9, 1929

February 8, 1940 — January 26, 1941

January 27, 1952 — February 13, 1953

February 13, 1964 — February 1, 1965

January 31, 1976 — February 17, 1977

February 17, 1988 — February 5, 1989

February 5, 2000 — January 23, 2001

HORSE

January 30, 1930 — February 16, 1931

February 15, 1942 — February 4, 1943

February 3, 1954 — January 23, 1955

January 21, 1966 — February 8, 1967

February 7, 1978 — January 27, 1979

January 27, 1990 — February 14, 1991

February 12, 2002 — January 31, 2003

SNAKE

February 10, 1929 — January 29, 1930

January 27, 1941 — February 14, 1942

February 14, 1953 — February 2, 1954

February 2, 1965 — January 20, 1966

February 18, 1977 — February 6, 1978

February 6, 1989 — January 26, 1990

January 24, 2001 — February 11, 2002

SHEEP

February 17, 1931 — February 5, 1932

February 5, 1943 — January 24, 1944

January 24, 1955 — February 11, 1956

February 9, 1967 — January 29, 1968

January 28, 1979 — February 15, 1980

February 15, 1991 — February 3, 1992

February 1, 2003 — January 21, 2004

MONKEY

February 6, 1932 — January 25, 1933

January 25, 1944 — February 12, 1945

February 12, 1956 — January 30, 1957

January 30, 1968 — February 16, 1969

February 16, 1980 — February 4, 1981

February 4, 1992 — January 22, 1993

January 22, 2004 — February 8, 2005

ROOSTER

January 26, 1933 — February 13, 1934

February 13, 1945 — February 1, 1946

January 31, 1957 — February 17, 1958

February 17, 1969 — February 5, 1970

February 5, 1981 — January 24, 1982

January 23, 1993 — February 9, 1994

February 9, 2005 — January 28, 2006

DOG

February 14, 1934 — February 3, 1935

February 2, 1946 — January 21, 1947

February 18, 1958 — February 7, 1959

February 6, 1970 — January 26, 1971

January 25, 1982 — February 12, 1983

February 10, 1994 — January 30, 1995

January 29, 2006 — February 17, 2007

PIG

February 4, 1935 — January 23, 1936

January 22, 1947 — February 9, 1948

February 8, 1959 — January 27, 1960

January 27, 1971 — February 14, 1972

February 13, 1983 — February 1, 1984

January 31, 1995 — February 18, 1996

February 18, 2007 — February 6, 2008

SEEKING A HAPPY LIFE

The spells, amulets, charms and talismans devised for money magic can buy you the time to work out the bigger picture of how your life is going, whether or not you should change direction, and the type of lifestyle you desire. Worrying about money or your financial circumstances can be one of the most overwhelming of experiences. This is because money and a strong sense of prosperity are emotionally linked to nurturing and supporting yourself and your family.

However, it is important to keep in mind that these aspects of life are merely beacons for a much stronger magic — the magic of being able to maximize control of your own destiny.

Whether you were born under a lucky star or are thrown in the deep end, being clear about some of the challenges that you need to face in life is important knowledge that can help you navigate a path for yourself, which allows you the richest possible life, not only in terms of money, but in terms of life experiences, friendships, love and integrity. Understand your destiny and then make plans to get the most out of it.

Learning to implement the basic lessons of magic will empower you to live your life with a sense of abundance and wonder at the beauty, balances and potential of the world around you. Nothing is impossible.

ANCIENT WISDOM

All human beings seek the happy life,
but many confuse the means — for example,
wealth and status — with life itself.
This misguided focus on the means to a good life
makes people get further from the happy life.
The really worthwhile things are the
virtuous activities that make up the happy life,
not the external means that may seem to produce it.
Epictetus, The Art of Living *(55 A.D.-135 A.D.)*

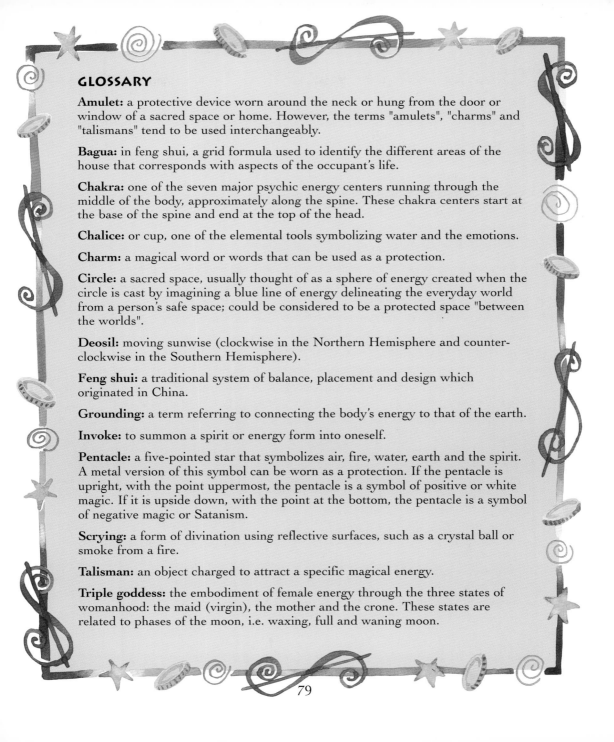

GLOSSARY

Amulet: a protective device worn around the neck or hung from the door or window of a sacred space or home. However, the terms "amulets", "charms" and "talismans" tend to be used interchangeably.

Bagua: in feng shui, a grid formula used to identify the different areas of the house that corresponds with aspects of the occupant's life.

Chakra: one of the seven major psychic energy centers running through the middle of the body, approximately along the spine. These chakra centers start at the base of the spine and end at the top of the head.

Chalice: or cup, one of the elemental tools symbolizing water and the emotions.

Charm: a magical word or words that can be used as a protection.

Circle: a sacred space, usually thought of as a sphere of energy created when the circle is cast by imagining a blue line of energy delineating the everyday world from a person's safe space; could be considered to be a protected space "between the worlds".

Deosil: moving sunwise (clockwise in the Northern Hemisphere and counter-clockwise in the Southern Hemisphere).

Feng shui: a traditional system of balance, placement and design which originated in China.

Grounding: a term referring to connecting the body's energy to that of the earth.

Invoke: to summon a spirit or energy form into oneself.

Pentacle: a five-pointed star that symbolizes air, fire, water, earth and the spirit. A metal version of this symbol can be worn as a protection. If the pentacle is upright, with the point uppermost, the pentacle is a symbol of positive or white magic. If it is upside down, with the point at the bottom, the pentacle is a symbol of negative magic or Satanism.

Scrying: a form of divination using reflective surfaces, such as a crystal ball or smoke from a fire.

Talisman: an object charged to attract a specific magical energy.

Triple goddess: the embodiment of female energy through the three states of womanhood: the maid (virgin), the mother and the crone. These states are related to phases of the moon, i.e. waxing, full and waning moon.

First published by Lansdowne Publishing Pty Ltd, 2000

This edition published in 2000 by
Parkgate Books
London House
Great Eastern Wharf
Parkgate Road
London SW11 4NQ
Great Britain

ISBN 1-902616-21-9

1 3 5 7 9 8 6 4 2

British Library Cataloguing-in-Publication Data:
A catalogue record for this book is available from the British Library.

Designer: Janet Marando
Illustrator: Sue Ninham

Set in Cochin on QuarkXPress
Printed in Singapore by Tien Wah Press (Pte) Ltd

Quotes from Epictetus are taken from a new interpretation by Sharon Lebell of
Epictetus works in *The Art of Living: The Classic Manual on Virtue, Happiness, and
Effectiveness,* published by HarperSan Francisco, 1995.